Tarquin Mathematical Challenges

An Alphabet of Tasks and Teasers

John Plant

tarquin

John Plant lives and works in Kent.

For many years, as a mathematics teacher and adviser, John has pursued his interest in problem solving, particularly by exploring the use of practical approaches.

Tarquin Mathematical Challenges is an extension to the excellent and best-selling series for able upper primary and lower secondary ages from Tarquin. Titles are:

The Number Detective	ISBN 978 1 899618 33 3
The Number Puzzler	ISBN 978 1 899618 47 3
Tarquin Number Challenges	ISBN 978 1 899618 49 1

These titles are part of the Tarquin commitment to enrichment of mathematics teaching. We have thousands of excellent products on our website to make teaching mathematics interesting - including:

- Books, for photocopying, for model-making and for ideas
- Posters
- Equipment - including dice, 360° protractors, Polydron and tessellations activities
- Materials from all around the world.

Keep up to date on Twitter, Facebook or by registering for our monthly newsletter through our website. There are lots of free resources, competitions and ideas to be found.

© John Plant 2014
ISBN 978-1-90755-029-4
Printed and designed in the UK

tarquin publications
Suite 74, 17 Holywell Hill
St Albans AL1 1DT, UK

www.tarquingroup.com

Tarquin Mathematical Challenges

An Alphabet of Tasks and Teasers

Introduction

The challenges in this book are mainly designed for able mathematicians in upper primary or lower secondary although many of the tasks are appropriate for a much wider range of ages.

Each task has a Task Sheet describing the challenge and Explanatory Notes that include learning objectives, resources implications, advice, answers and possible further study.

The challenges are graded in terms of their accessibility to a wide range of ability (rather than in terms of difficulty) as follows:

★   Largely practical and very accessible to a wide range of ability with pupils able to achieve success at different levels. The challenges often involve investigation requiring limited specialist mathematical knowledge although full completion of the tasks can be difficult.

★★   Less accessible because the problem solving involves significant analysis and some specialist mathematical knowledge. Some may find these tasks frustrating because they cannot find the solutions.

★★★   Very challenging tasks that require substantial mathematical thinking and use of significant specialist knowledge.

Many of the challenges are presented as practical problems to help pupils develop their mathematical thinking. These tasks involve the use of basic classroom equipment such as linking cubes, counters, ruler & compasses etc. The following specialist paper resources and mastersheets are provided at the end of the book:

Maze Grids	*Sudoku Grid*	*Star Grid*
Number Clocks	*Squared paper*	*Dotty isometric paper*

Most of the challenges are suitable for paired or group work, thus promoting mathematical discussion and the sharing of ideas. A certificate of Achievement is provided at the end of the book for rewarding pupils on the successful completion of a task.

Contents

		Tasks	Accessibility	Page
Alpha	α	Cubes Investigation	★	4
Beta	β	Two Cards	★★	6
Gamma	γ	Target Number Challenge	★	8
Delta	δ	Detective Work	★★★	10
Epsilon	ε	Tri-Flake	★★★	12
Zeta	ζ	Question Mark	★★	14
Eta	η	Riddle Me!	★★	16
Theta	θ	Question of Balance	★	18
Iota	ι	Maze Corridor	★	20
Kappa	κ	Where in the World?	★★	22
Lambda	λ	Water Works	★★★	24
Mu	μ	Nesting	★	26
Nu	ν	Lunchboxes	★★	28
Xi	ξ	Roman Numbers	★★	30
Omicron	ο	Products	★★	32
Pi	π	Sudo-Colours	★★	34
Rho	ρ	Domino Dilemma	★	36
Sigma	σ	Trihexs	★	38
Tau	τ	Sticky Problem	★★★	40
Upsilon	υ	Star Grid	★★	42
Phi	φ	Circle Search	★★★	44
Chi	χ	Tessellating Ts	★	46
Psi	ψ	Cups and Saucers	★★	48
Omega	Ω	Number Clocks	★★	50
		Mastersheets including *Folding Instructions* & *Code Dial*		52
		Mathematical papers		59
		Certificate of Achievement		

downloadable from www.tarquingroup.com - quick search Plant

Challenge α (alpha)
Cubes Investigation

Use 4 linking cubes of the same colour.
Join them to make this solid shape.

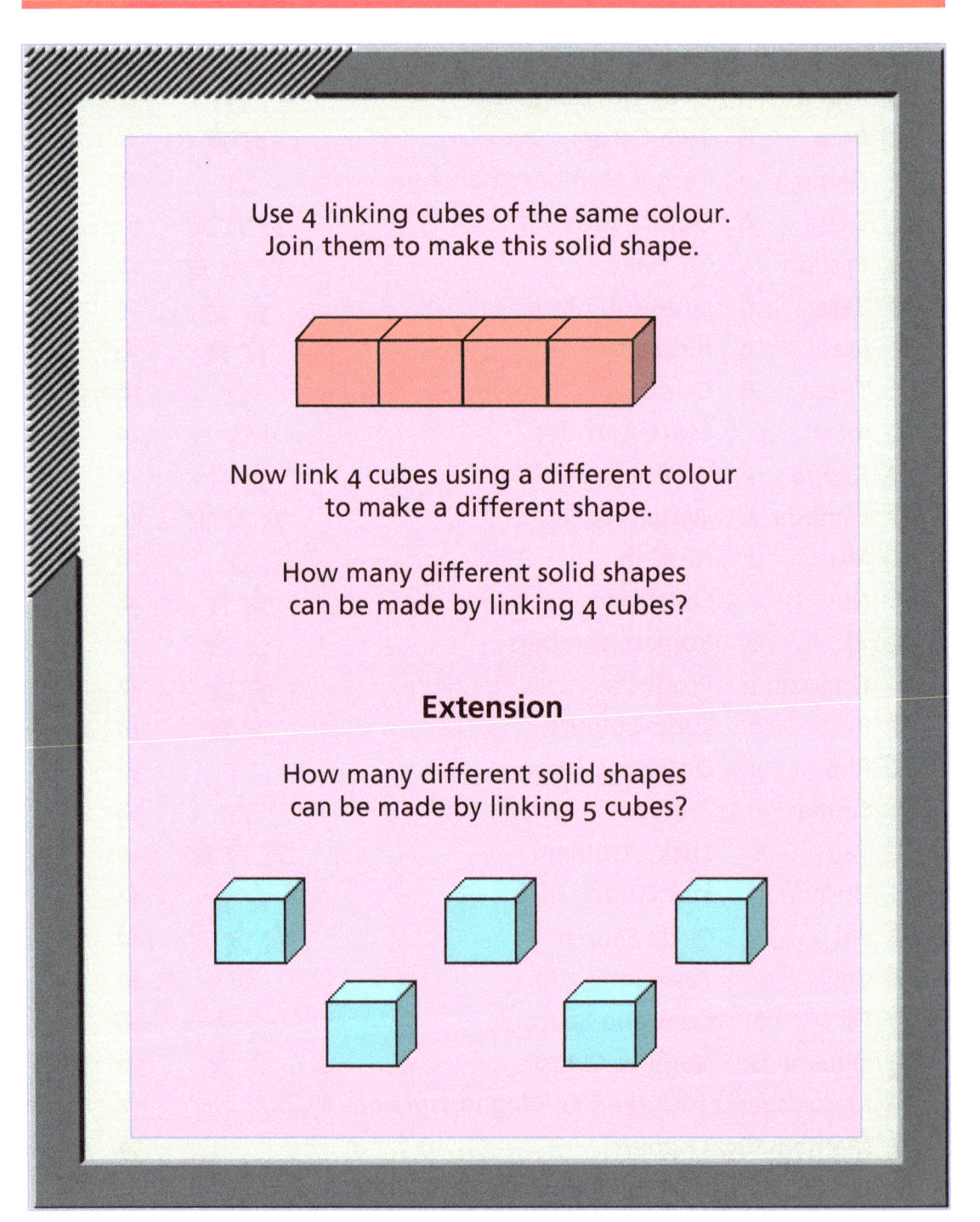

Now link 4 cubes using a different colour
to make a different shape.

How many different solid shapes
can be made by linking 4 cubes?

Extension

How many different solid shapes
can be made by linking 5 cubes?

Explanatory Notes: Cubes Investigation

Materials: linking cubes, plain, squared or isometric paper (see pages 59/ 60)
Objectives: to visualise and record solid shapes, recognising congruent shapes and reflected pairs

There are 8 different shapes that can be made by joining together 4 linking cubes. Five of them lie 'flat' just one cube high.

Here, some pupils may have duplicates having failed to recognise congruency.

Three more cannot be laid flat and here there is a right and left handed pair.

It is interesting to see which pupils extend their thinking in this new direction. Initially pupils may have difficulty distinguishing between the reflected pair.

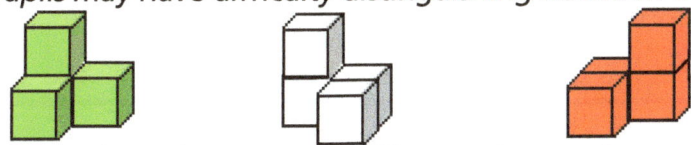

With 5 cubes, there are 12 different shapes that can be laid flat. These represent the 12 pentominoes.

Pupils could build all 12 shapes with cubes. Alternatively, given only 5 cubes, pupils could be asked to record their shapes on paper. This is a good task for developing partner or group work. Pupils begin the investigation individually before joining forces to share results and produce one set of shapes between them.

There are a further 17 shapes of 5 cubes that cannot be laid flat.

Here, pupils may begin to devise strategies for finding them all. For example: 5-cube shapes can be formed by adding an extra cube to 4-cube shapes.

Further Study

Pupils might like to
- *investigate 6-cube shapes*
- *find different ways of recording their work*
- *investigate pentomino puzzles*

Challenge β (beta)
Two Cards

Cut a 12 cm by 12 cm square of card into two pieces like this:

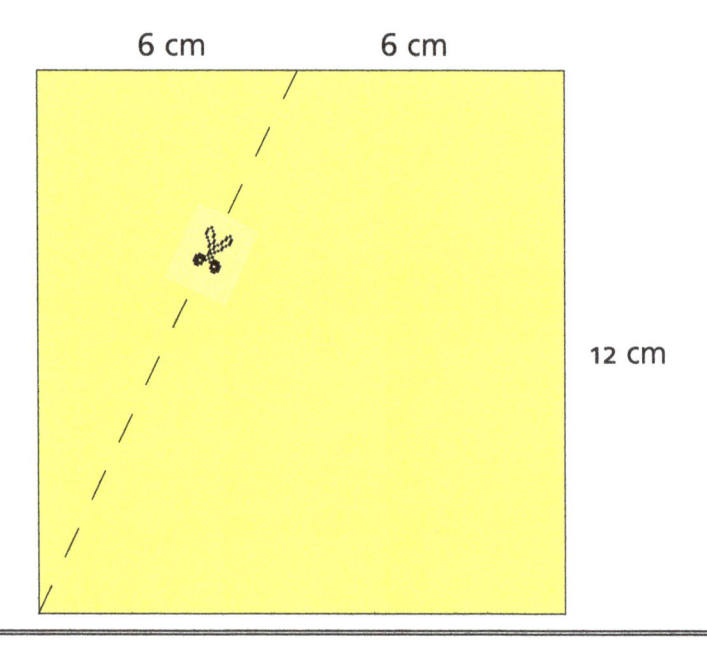

6 cm   6 cm

12 cm

Joining together the two pieces can make different shapes.
The two pieces must be joined along 'matching' sides.

Matching sides must have the same length.
There must be no overlapping.

Clearly, the pieces can be joined back together to form a square.

What other polygons can you make by joining matching sides?

Extension

If a circle can be drawn so that it passes through each of the vertices
of a polygon
then the polygon is called **cyclic**.

Which of the polygons you made are cyclic?

For each one, find the radius of the circle.

Explanatory Notes: Two Cards

Materials: card, scissors, compasses & pencil, ruler
Objectives: to recognise and name some geometric shapes; to draw circles and measure the radii

There are 8 different geometric shapes that can be formed by matching sides. There is one triangle, four quadrilaterals and three pentagons.

With only one set of cards, pupils will need to record each one they find. Note: the parallelogram is not a rhombus.

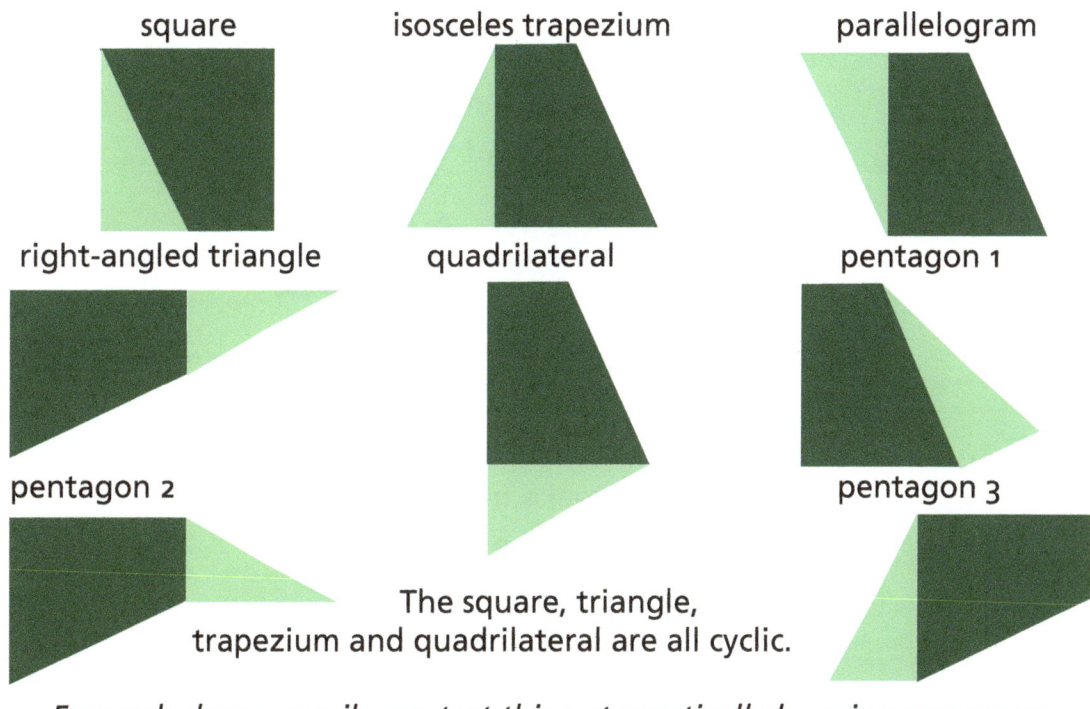

square   isosceles trapezium   parallelogram

right-angled triangle   quadrilateral   pentagon 1

pentagon 2   pentagon 3

The square, triangle, trapezium and quadrilateral are all cyclic.

For each shape, pupils can test this out practically by using compasses to draw the circle that passes through all of the vertices.
They can then measure the radius of each circle (to 1 decimal place).
Square (8.5 cm); Triangle (19.0 cm); Trapezium (9.5 cm); Quadrilateral (9.5 cm)

The radii can be calculated exactly.

Square ($6\sqrt{2}$ cm); Triangle ($6\sqrt{10}$ cm); Trapezium ($3\sqrt{10}$ cm); Quadrilateral ($3\sqrt{10}$ cm)

Challenge γ (gamma)
Target Number Challenge

How many of the first 30 whole numbers
can you calculate by combining
in different ways the numbers

2, 3, 18 and ½?

Each calculation must use
all four numbers (once only)
and any combination of +, −, × or ÷

For example: 16 = (½ × 2) + (18 − 3)

Extension

How many of the first 30 whole numbers
can you make from just
2, 3 and 18 ?

Each calculation must use
all three numbers (once only)
and any combination of +, −, × or ÷

You may also use powers.

Explanatory Notes: Target Number Challenge

Materials: scientific calculator
Objectives: to calculate using the four rules and brackets

The answers below are not unique solutions. There may be alternative solutions or different ways of expressing the same calculations. Brackets have been used to emphasise the order of calculation although under the rules of algebraic logic they are not always needed. *This might be an opportunity to introduce pupils to algebraic logic of a scientific calculator, allowing them to explore the need for brackets. The use of powers can offer further solutions. The numbers 2, 3 & ½ can be used as indices.*

1 =	(18 × ½) ÷ 3 - 2		16 =	(2 × ½) + 18 - 3
2 =	(18 ÷ 3) - (2 ÷ ½)		17 =	(18 + 3) - (2 ÷ ½)
3 =	(18 × ½) - (2 × 3)		18 =	(2 ÷ ½ - 3) × 18
4 =	(18 × ½) - (3 + 2)		19 =	(2 ÷ ½) + 18 - 3
5 =	(18 × ½) ÷ 3 + 2		20 =	(18 + 3) - (2 × ½)
6 =	(18 × ½) ÷ 3 × 2		21 =	(18 × ½ - 2) × 3
7 =	(18 ÷ 3) + (2 × ½)		22 =	(2 × ½) + 3 + 18
8 =	(18 × ½) + 2 - 3		23 =	(3 - ½) × 2 + 18
9 =	(18 × ½) × (3 - 2)		24 =	(18 × ½ + 3) × 2
10 =	(18 × ½) + 3 - 2		25 =	(18 × ½) × 3 - 2
11 =	(18 + 3) ÷ 2 + ½		26 =	(3 ÷ ½) + 2 + 18
12 =	(3 ÷ ½ + 18) ÷ 2		27 =	(3 + ½ - 2) × 18
13 =	(18 ÷ 3 + ½) × 2		28 =	(3 × 18 + 2) × ½
14 =	(18 × ½) + 2 + 3		29 =	(18 × ½ × 3) + 2
15 =	(18 ÷ ½) ÷ 2 - 3		30 =	(18 ÷ ½) - (2 × 3)

Extension

1 =	$(3-2)^{18}$	9 =	$18 - 3^2$	19 =	18 + 3 - 2
2 =	$\dfrac{18}{3^2}$	10 =	$18 - 2^3$	23 =	18 + 3 + 2
3 =	$\dfrac{18}{2 \times 3}$	12 =	18 - (3 × 2)	24 =	18 + (3 × 2)
4 =	(18 ÷ 3) - 2	13 =	18 - 3 - 2	26 =	$18 + 2^3$
6 =	(18 ÷ 2) - 3	17 =	18 + 2 - 3	27 =	$18 + 3^2$
8 =	(18 ÷ 3) + 2	18 =	18 (3 - 2)	30 =	2 (18 - 3)

Challenge δ (delta)
Detective Work

I have been given this strange question!

ITNJT   PMZCOL   KCXFCX   FADAJDNYA

FAJNQTASAF   LAJSAD   ZALLMWAL

DC   LCKYA   DTA   ZELDASE

CP   DTA   FMXJNXW   ZAX ?

Can anyone answer it for me?

Extension

Give your answer in the code.
You might find it helpful to use
the Code Dial.

Explanatory Notes: Detective Work

Materials: Mastersheet: Code Dial (page 52), split pin
Objectives: to understand and use a letter-substitution code

The message reads:

Which famous London detective
deciphered secret messages
to solve the mystery
of the dancing men ?

This is a reference to 'The Adventure of the Dancing Men'
a story in 'The Return of Sherlock Holmes'
by Sir Arthur Conan Doyle.

The answer to the question is

SHERLOCK HOLMES

*Pupils may need some clues to help them decode the message.
The question mark gives a clue to the first word; the 2-letter and
3-letter words are worth investigating; in the English language,
E is the most common letter.
Pupils may enjoy reading 'The Adventure of the Dancing Men'.*

To write the answer 'Sherlock Holmes' in code, pupils will need to
construct and complete the Code Dial on the page 52.
(This will reveal the code for the letter K.)

The coded answer is

LTASKCJG TCKZAL

Further study

*Pupils may enjoy sending one another messages using the Code Dial
or inventing codes of their own.*

Challenge ε (epsilon)
Tri-flake

This tri-flake is made from equilateral triangles.
Smaller triangles **trisect** the sides of larger ones like this.
The largest triangle has a perimeter of 3 units.

What is the perimeter of this tri-flake?

Explanatory Notes: Tri-flake

Materials: plain paper, ruler, compasses
Objectives: to trisect lengths in order to build a fractal shape

The tri-flake is a fractal pattern formed in stages, beginning with an equilateral triangle. Further stages are constructed by tri-secting (dividing into 3 equal parts) the sides of triangles and building on new similar triangles of a third of the length.

In each stage of the fractal process the perimeter of the developing shape increases by the factor 4/3.

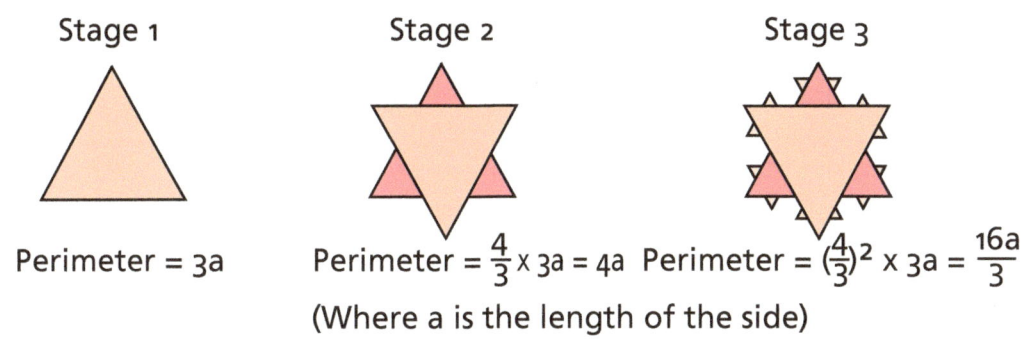

Stage 1   Stage 2   Stage 3

Perimeter = 3a   Perimeter = $\frac{4}{3}$ × 3a = 4a   Perimeter = $(\frac{4}{3})^2$ × 3a = $\frac{16a}{3}$

(Where a is the length of the side)

The pupils are shown stage 4, given the length of side as 3 units and asked for the perimeter which equals $\frac{64a}{9}$ = $21\frac{1}{3}$ units.

(Note: if the area of the original triangle is 1 unit² then the area of the next three stages are: $\frac{4}{3}$ unit²; $\frac{40}{27}$ unit²; $\frac{376}{243}$ unit²)

Pupils may like to construct this fractal using a large sheet of plain paper, ruler and compasses. A good starting point is an equilateral triangle of side 18cm or 27cm which can be constructed using ruler & compasses only. Once the sides have been trisected, following stages can be constructed using lines parallel to the sides of the original triangle.

Further study

How many stages can the fractal pattern have?
How long can the perimeter get?
What happens to the area of the pattern as it moves through stages?

The fractal can grow infinitely. Since every stage increases the perimeter by a third, then the perimeter can become infinitely long. Clearly the area also increases at each stage but there is a finite limit to the area.

Challenge ζ (zeta)
Question Mark

Take a set of playing cards Ace – 9.

Lay them out in a question mark pattern like this.

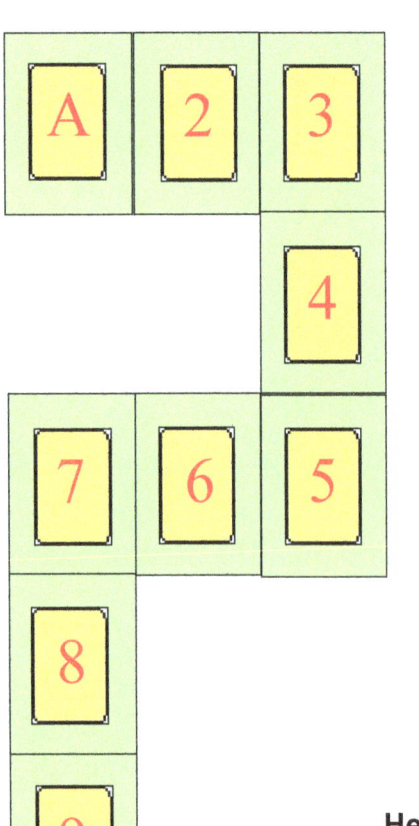

Count Ace = 1

This question mark pattern has

two rows of 3 cards
(A + 2 + 3 = 6   and   5 + 6 + 7 = 18)

and

two columns of 3 cards
(3 + 4 + 5 = 12   and   7 + 8 + 9 = 24)

The total of each row and column is a **different multiple of 6**.
(6, 18, 12 and 24)

Here is the problem

Rearrange the cards so that
the total of each row and column
is the **same prime number**.

Explanatory Notes: Question Mark

Materials: playing cards or numbered cards 1-9
Objectives: to solve a numerical puzzle involving multiples and prime numbers

Solution 1 for the prime number 13   Solution 2 for the prime number 17

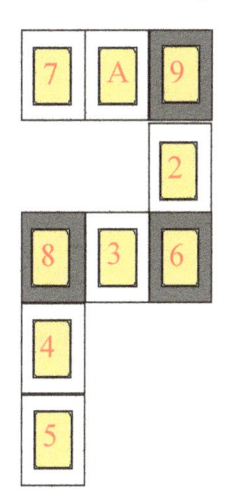

There are variations to the solutions above. Some numbers can be swapped, for example, the numbers 5 & 6 in solution 1. Other numbers have to be in particular squares. Pupils might investigate the variations.

Strategy

The problem can be solved analytically as follows:

- The 9 numbers add up to 45
- Three of the cards (at the corners) must appear in a row *and* a column
- These 3 corner cards will count twice so the total sum of the 2 rows and 2 columns must be greater than 45
- The total of all the rows and columns must be 4 x a prime number
- 4 x 11 = 44 (too small) but 4 x 19 = 76 (too big)
- Try 13, total must be 4 x 13 = 52, so the 3 corner cards must add up to 52 − 45 = 7
- Corner cards can only be A, 2 & 4
- Use a similar approach for prime number 17.

Challenge η (eta)
Riddle Me!

Warm Up

These cards give 4 clues to a secret number.

| I am less than 20 | I am an odd number | I am a multiple of 3 | I am more than 10 |

Work out the secret number.

Riddle

Now look at these six clues.

| I am a square number | I am an even number | I am a cube number |

| I am a 3-digit number | I am less than 500 | I am a multiple of 27 |

Prove that there is no number for which all six clues are true.

For what numbers are 5 of the six clues true?

Explanatory Notes: Riddle Me!

Materials: cards, scissors, envelope (optional)
Objectives: to solve numerical problems with odd even, square & cube numbers
Warm Up: The solution is 15
Riddle: There are 7 cube numbers less than 500 (1, 8, 27, 64, 125, 216, 343) but none of these satisfy all the other 5 conditions as shown in the table below. This proves that there is *no* number for which all 6 clues are true:

Cube	Less than 500	3-digit	Even	Square	Multiple of 27
1	Y	X	X	Y	X
8	Y	X	Y	X	X
27	Y	X	X	X	Y
64	Y	X	Y	Y	X
125	Y	Y	X	X	X
216	Y	Y	Y	X	Y
343	Y	Y	X	X	X
512	X	Y	Y	X	X
729	X	Y	X	Y	Y

However 216 is a cube number for which 5 of the clues are true.

Any other number satisfying 5 conditions must be a 3-digit, even, square number.

Square	Less than 500	3-digit	Even	Cube	Multiple of 27
100	Y	Y	Y	X	X
144	Y	Y	Y	X	X
196	Y	Y	Y	X	X
256	Y	Y	Y	X	X
324	Y	Y	Y	X	Y
400	Y	Y	Y	X	X
484	Y	Y	Y	X	X
576	X	Y	Y	X	X
676	X	Y	Y	X	X
784	X	Y	Y	X	X
900	X	Y	Y	X	X

This gives a second solution of 324.

The two tasks can be presented as 'envelope' puzzles by printing the clues on cards and putting them in an envelope with the questions on the front.

Challenge θ (theta)
Question of Balance

Four rods are stacked at the edge of a table.

The rods are balanced on top on one another so that they reach **beyond** the edge of the table.

Each rod is a cuboid measuring 2cm by 2cm by 24 cm.

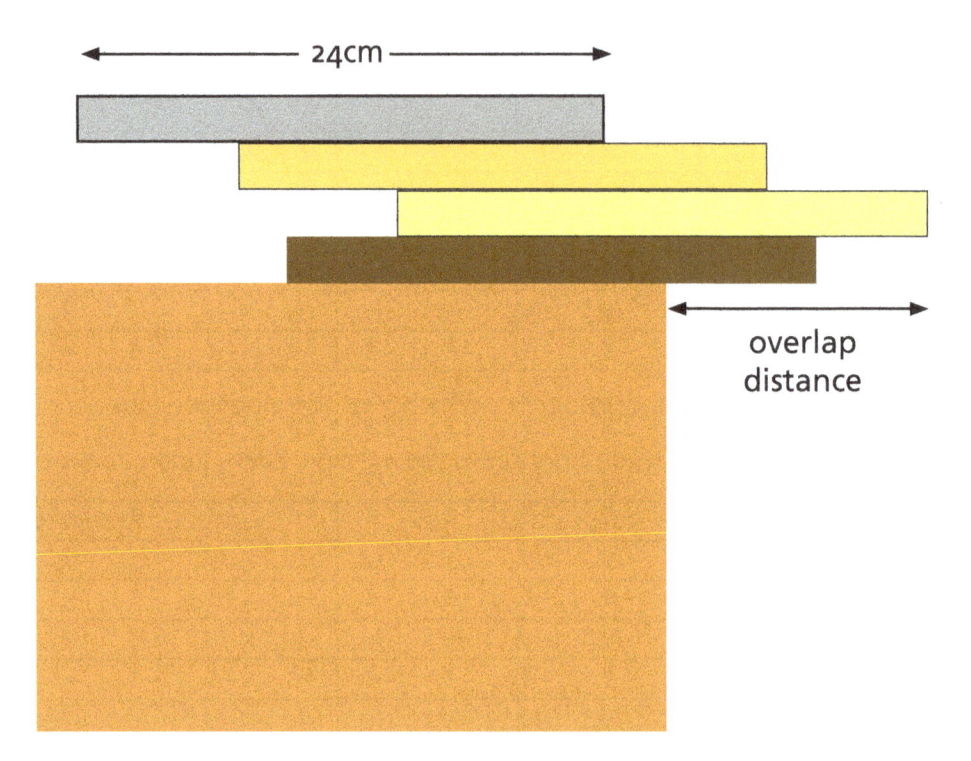

←——— 24cm ———→

overlap distance

What is the maximum possible *overlap distance* that can be achieved by rearranging the rods?

*The rods must remain horizontal.
They must all lie parallel to one another.*

Explanatory Notes: Question of Balance

Materials: four rods of length 24 cm built using linking cubes

Objectives: to investigate equilibrium and recognise rotational forces

The task is intended as an experimental practical activity in which pupils investigate the nature of balancing rotational forces. In the context of the task, pupils need to be clear that the rods must remain parallel and horizontal. Pupils may need to develop an appropriate vocabulary to discuss their work including terms such as centre of gravity, equilibrium, tipping point, stable & unstable.

The rods can be arranged to reach out beyond the length of a rod. In this example each layer is on the point of tipping and the overlap distances between the rods are 12cm, 6cm, 4cm, and 3cm giving a total of 25cm.

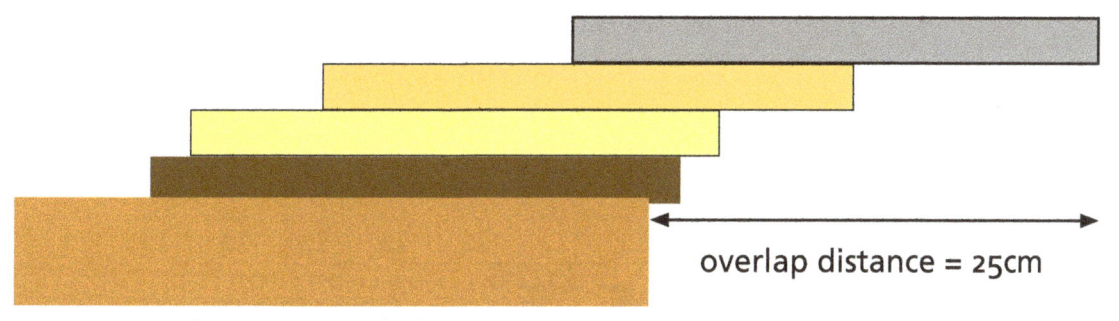

overlap distance = 25cm

By using rods as counterbalances, the overlap can be increased as in this example where the two overlaps are 12cm & 15cm.

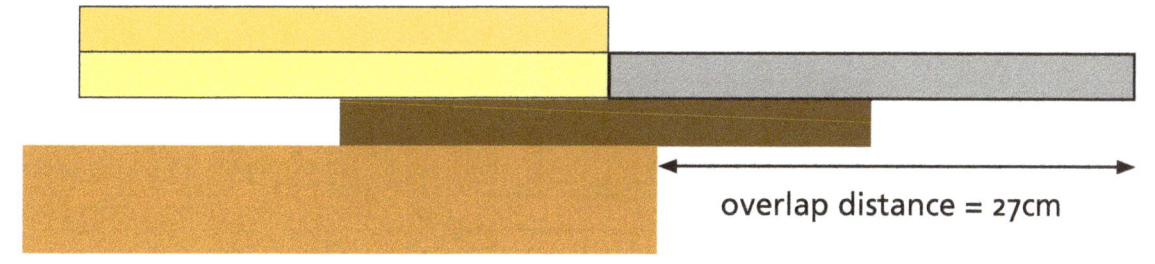

overlap distance = 27cm

Further Study

During the task the concept of a turning force or the moment of a force could be introduced i.e. it is not just how much of a rod is on one side of a point of balance but how far away its centre of gravity is from the point. The balancing moments of forces can be illustrated using the two examples above.

Challenge ι (iota)
Maze Corridor

On a 6 by 6 grid, choose a starting square. Label it **S**

Move around the grid to form a corridor. Label the last square **F**

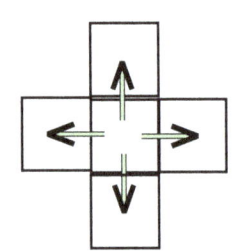

You are only allowed to move to a square that is horizontally or vertically adjacent. You cannot move diagonally.

You are not allowed to visit any square more than once.
By filling in squares, you must design a route that is one square wide and which does not meet itself.

From start to finish, this route is 20 squares long.

Find the longest possible route.

Explanatory Notes: Maze Corridor

Materials: Mastersheet: Maze Grids (page 53), cubes (optional)
Objectives: to investigate the arrangement of a 6x6 maze noting significant design features

Features to note are that good use is made of side squares and, particularly corner squares and that two path squares are allowed to touch at the corner which helps to maximise the corridor. On a 6x6 grid, a maze corridor of 24 squares can be designed as shown in the example below.

This investigation can be done more practically by placing cubes on a grid.

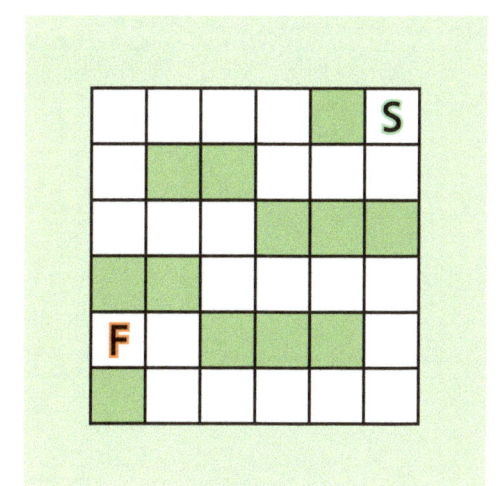

*A possible approach to encourage pupils is to set targets.
Bronze = 21 squares; Silver = 22 squares; Gold = 23 or more squares*

Further Study

Pupils might like to try the problem on a 7x7 grid with the following targets:

Bronze = 28 squares; Silver = 30 squares; Gold = 32 or more squares

From start to finish, this route is 33 squares long.

Challenge κ (kappa)
Where in the world?

COVE BAY
LAT 51° 26' 39"N
LONG 0° 22' 25"E

Where in the world is this?
What is the name of the cove?
What is the name of the bay?

Explanatory Notes: Where in the world?

Materials: access to the internet

Objectives: to identify a geographical location using latitude and longitude

This is a research task that involves using internet search features.
The location is by the River Thames at Gravesend in Kent.
It inscription reads Anchor Cove, Bawley Bay.

Here is an opportunity to introduce pupils to:
- The use of latitude and longitude to identify and locate position on the surface of the Earth
- The angles that produce the values of latitude & longitude
- The use of degrees, minutes and seconds as units of measure of angles
- The significance of Greenwich and the Prime Meridian line
- The link between longitude and time zones across the world

Pupils might need to consider what size of area is covered by the given latitude and longitude.

Pupils may like to plot the latitude and longitude of their school or their homes.

Further Study

The history of longitude is fascinating and its story is brilliantly described in Dava Sobel's book *Longitude* and was the subject of a 4-part TV series entitled 'Longitude' and still available on DVD. Both are usually availabe from Tarquin. *Longitude* tells the naval and scientific history of how astronomers and clockmakers competed to try to find a way of calculating the accurate position of a ship at sea. The story focuses on the life of John Harrison and the development of his sea clocks.

Greenwich is the focus on much of the history and Harrison's clocks are housed and displayed at the Royal Observatory in Greenwich. For scientific and historical reasons, longitude and time are linked with Greenwich in London as it was chosen as the site of the Prime Meridian (the zero longitude that separates the Eastern hemisphere from the Western hemisphere) and the basis of world time through Greenwich Mean Time (GMT). Visitors can walk across the Meridian Line at Greenwich and it is visible at night as a laser beam stretching across London.

Challenge λ (lambda)
Water Works

The jug contains 36 centilitres of water.

Water is poured into the top of the apparatus. At each of the junctions **X** & **Y** the water divides equally (one half goes left, the other half goes right).

The water is delivered into 3 beakers **A**, **B** & **C** at the bottom. Each beaker holds 20 centilitres (cl).

How can you use the apparatus so that the beakers contain:

a) 6cl, 12cl and 18cl

b) 12cl, 12cl and 12cl ?

You are only allowed to use the equipment given (no extra beaker!). The jug can be used to collect the water instead of one of the beakers. The water runs through the apparatus too quickly to allow the jug or a beaker to be used to pour the water at the top and then be moved to the bottom to collect. **Both problems can be solved.**

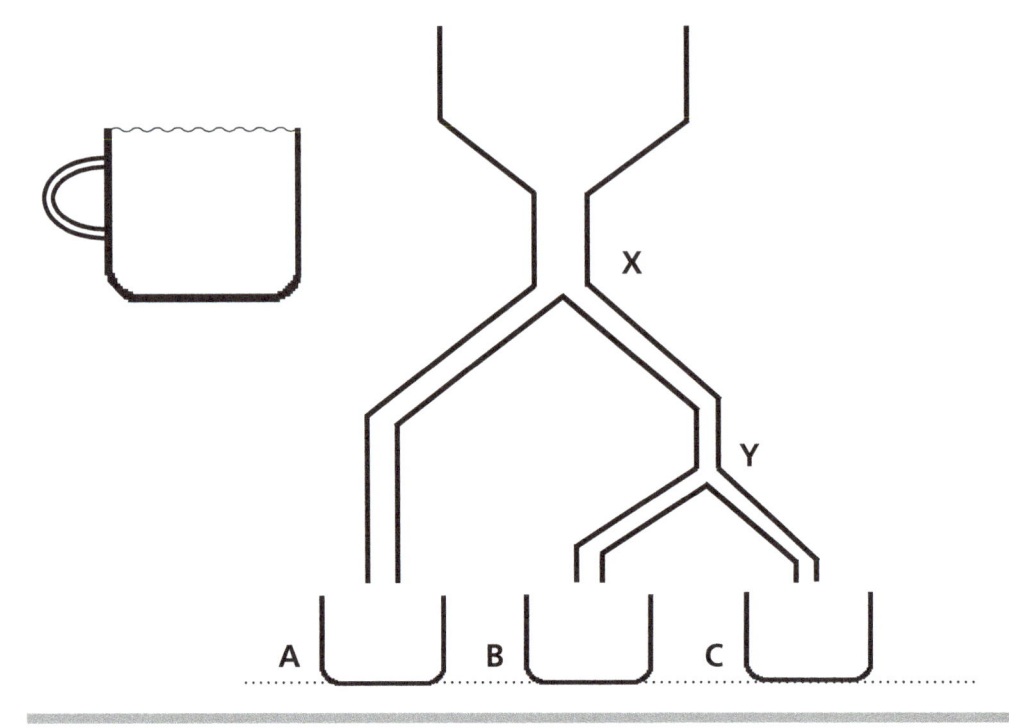

Explanatory Notes: Water Works

Materials: none
Objectives: to solve a numerical puzzle involving strategy and lateral thinking

Both problems can be solved using only the equipment provided.
Pupils may need to be reassured about this. There is no trickery involved.
Pupils may need assuring that there is no trick, the solutions (particularly the solution to b) require some clever thinking.

This kind of problem is not for everyone. Some will find it simply frustrating and quickly give up. For others it will be a challenge that they must solve and they will be relentless in their pursuit of a solution. One approach that can be useful is to start with the desired outcome and work backwards. The solutions below may not be unique.

a) To get 6cl, 12cl & 18cl

Actions	Jug	Beaker A	Beaker B	Beaker C
Start	36	0	0	0
Empty the jug into the apparatus	0	18	9	9
Fill beaker A from B	0	20	7	9
Empty beaker A into jug	20	0	7	9
Empty jug into apparatus	0	10	12	14
Empty beakers A & C into jug	24	0	12	0
Enpty jug into apparatus	0	12	18	6

b) To get 12cl, 12cl & 12cl

Actions	Jug	Beaker A	Beaker B	Beaker C
Start	36	0	0	0
Fill beaker A from the jug	16	20	0	0
Empty jug into beaker B	0	20	16	0
Empty beaker A into jug	20	0	16	0
Replace beaker A with the jug	20	0	16	0
Replace beaker B with beaker A	20	0	16	0
Empty beaker B into the apparatus	28	4	0	4
Empty beaker C into beaker A	28	8	0	0
Move beakers back to their original positions	28	8	0	0
Pour just enough water from the jug to apparatus so that beaker A is full	4	20	6	6
Empty beaker A into jug	24	0	6	6
Empty jug into apparatus	0	12	12	12

Challenge μ (mu)
Nesting

Use a sheet of A4 coloured paper.
Follow the folding instructions.
Make this (A4) kite.

Using two colours
Make 4 kites to form this pattern

Cut A4 paper in half to make A5 sheets
Follow the same folding instructions
Use your two colours
Make some A5 Kites
Glue them onto the A4 kites

Cut A5 paper in half to make A6 sheets
Follow the same folding instructions
Make some A6 Kites
Add them to your pattern

Repeat the process.
to make A7 and A8 Kites.
Add to your pattern
How small can you go?

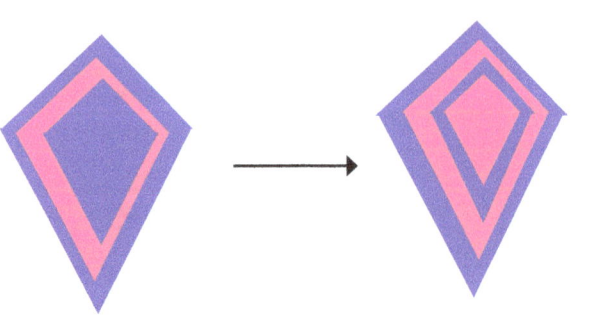

Explanatory Notes: Nesting

Materials: Mastersheets: Kite, (see page 54) and Equilateral Triangle (see page 55) A4 paper in a range of colours, glue, scissors, sellotape

Objectives: to recognise similarity, and create mathematical designs using similar shapes

This task involves making nesting patterns from kites, equilateral triangles or both. The shapes are made by folding standard sized sheets of paper (A3, A4, A5, A6 etc).

The folding instructions for the kite and for the equilateral triangle are provided at pages 54-55. Note: the folding instructions only work for paper of standard sizes (A1, A2, A3, A4, A5 etc).

Since the standard paper sizes are all mathematically similar then the families of folded kites and equilateral triangles are also similar. As the size of the shapes decreases, each new shape is half the area of the previous one.

For the kite, two of the angles are 45° and 90° which allows 4 kites or 8 kites to be joined together. Some ideas for creating nesting patterns for the kite are shown on the task page.

Pupils enjoy the creativity of this task, particularly trying to make shapes that are as small as possible. This gives them an experience of an infinite sequence.

Using larger sizes is also good fun (A4, A3, A2, A1)

Pupils should be encouraged to create imaginative nesting pattern designs. Using two or more colours is very effective.

It is possible to join together 2-D designs to create 3-D shapes such as a tetrahedron and square-based pyramid.

Challenge *v* (nu)
Lunchboxes

1. Amy, Billy, Chloe, Dev and Emma each own a lunchbox

2. The lunchboxes are standing in a straight line in the dining hall

3. Each lunchbox is a different colour

4. Each lunchbox contains a sandwich, a drink and a piece of fruit

5. Each child has a different sandwich, a different drink and a different fruit

The question is "Who has a pear for lunch?'

Facts:
The middle lunchbox is red
The banana is in the cola drinker's lunchbox
Dev has a cheese sandwich
There is a jam sandwich in the green lunchbox
The box with the egg sandwich is next to the one with the tuna sandwich
The peach belongs to Amy
The lunchbox with the orange is on the left of the box with the apple
Billy's lunchbox is next to the red one
The owner of the ham sandwich only drinks water
The blackcurrant drink is in the blue lunchbox
Emma's lunchbox is yellow
Chloe drinks lemonade
The milk is in the same lunchbox as the egg sandwich
The green lunchbox is on the left of the white one
There is a ham sandwich in the first lunchbox

Explanatory Notes: Lunchboxes

Materials: recording table (optional), set of attribute cards (optional)
Objectives: to analyse a set of facts to make correct deductions

The solution to the problem is Chloe. (She has the pear.)

The full details of the lunchboxes are as follows.

	Box 1	Box 2	Box 3	Box 4	Box 5
Name	Emma	Billy	Amy	Chloe	Dev
Colour	Yellow	Blue	Red	Green	White
Drink	Water	Blackcurrant	Milk	Lemonade	Cola
Sandwich	Ham	Tuna	Egg	Jam	Cheese
Fruit	Orange	Apple	Peach	Pear	Banana

The solution to the problem involves applying the given facts in the appropriate order. It also involves trying and eliminating unsuccessful options.

A recording table such as the one above can help pupils record the results of their analysis.

The problem could be made more practical by using cards labelled with the different attributes for pupils to sort. In this way they can deal more easily with errors and dead ends,

Challenge ξ (xi)
Roman Numbers

These pictures show numbers expressed in Roman Numerals.

Find the sum of all of the numbers shown.

Express your answer in Roman Numerals.

A.D. MDCCCXIV

XXIX MILES from LONDON Bridge

Explanatory Notes: Roman Numbers

Materials: none
Objectives: to understand and use Roman numerals

The numbers shown are:

    Clockface totals = 78

    XXIX = 29 (miles from London Bridge)

    MDCCCXIV = 1814 (date on building)

The sum

    = 78 + 78 + 29 + 1814

    = 1999

    = MCMXCIX (not MIM)

The number 4 is usually shown on clockfaces as IIII (not IV). This is done to give the clockface a greater look of symmetry with the IIII opposite the VIII.

Pupils may not be familiar with Roman numerals and may need to be introduced to the basic numerals.

I = 1	V = 5	X = 10	
L = 50	C = 100	D = 500	M = 1000

They may need to practice making numbers, particularly recognising that

4 = IV	40 = XL	90 = XC
400 = CD	900 = CM	

Further Study

Pupils might like to investigate further than use of Roman Numerals and perhaps take their own photographs showing examples.

Challenge o (omicron)
Products

The **sum** of the first 5 consecutive whole numbers is 15

| 1 | + | 2 | + | 3 | + | 4 | + | 5 | = | 15 |

Find 5 consecutive whole numbers with a **sum** of 1515

| | + | | + | | + | | + | | = | 1515 |

The **product** of the first 5 consecutive whole numbers is 120

| 1 | × | 2 | × | 3 | × | 4 | × | 5 | = | 120 |

Find 5 consecutive whole numbers with a **product** of 360360

| | × | | × | | × | | × | | = | 360360 |

Find 5 whole numbers with a product of 5105100 where the **difference** between the largest and the smallest is less than 10

| | × | | × | | × | | × | | = | 5105100 |

Explanatory Notes: Products

Materials: none
Objectives: to understand and use the terms 'sum', 'product' and 'difference' and to calculate sums and products

This is a non-calculator task.

Solutions are:

| 301 | + | 302 | + | 303 | + | 304 | + | 305 | = | 1515 |

| 11 | × | 12 | × | 13 | × | 14 | × | 15 | = | 360360 |

| 17 | × | 21 | × | 22 | × | 25 | × | 26 | = | 5105100 |

Strategies

The first problem can be solved using the given information at the sum of the first 5 whole numbers is 15. For the required total of 1515 less the 15 leaves 1500 to find from the 5 missing numbers (300 each).

The product of the first 5 whole numbers gives a clue to the solution to the second problem using factors.

$$
\begin{aligned}
360360 &= 120 \times 3003 \\
&= (2 \times 3 \times 4 \times 5) \times (3 \times 1001) \\
&= 2 \times 3 \times 4 \times 5 \times 3 \times 11 \times 91 \\
&= 2 \times 3 \times 4 \times 5 \times 3 \times 11 \times 7 \times 13 \\
&= 11 \times (3 \times 4) \times 13 \times (2 \times 7) \times (3 \times 5) \\
&= 11 \times 12 \times 13 \times 14 \times 15
\end{aligned}
$$

The method of factors can also be successfully deployed for the third problem.

Challenge π (pi)
Sudo-colours

For this practical puzzle, you need:
81 cubes (or counters) - 9 each of 9 different colours.
a blank 9 by 9 'Sudoku' grid- made from nine 3 by 3 squares.

For your starting position, place cubes on your grid as shown below.

Y = yellow; B = blue, BK = black, BR = brown, G = green, R = red, P = pink, O = orange, W = white

	Y	O		BK				B
		G		B			R	
	P				Y		W	
		R	BR					BK
	G		BK			BR		
BR					O		G	P
	BK		W		R			
O		B		P				
W	R					O	Y	

Complete the grid so that each row, each column and each 3 by 3 square contains one cube (or counter) of each of the nine colours.

Explanatory Notes: Sudo-colours

Materials: Mastersheet: Sudoku Grid (see page 56), 81 cubes (or counters) - 9 each of 9 different colours.
Objectives: to complete Sudoku puzzle practically using coloured cubes

The puzzle is presented in a practical way so that it is tactile and can be tackled individually or by a small collaborative group. The solution as follows.

R	Y	O	P	BK	W	G	BR	B
BK	W	G	O	B	BR	P	R	Y
B	P	BR	G	R	Y	BK	W	O
Y	O	R	BR	G	P	W	B	BK
P	G	W	BK	Y	B	BR	O	R
BR	B	BK	R	W	O	Y	G	P
G	BK	Y	W	O	R	B	P	BR
O	BR	B	Y	P	G	R	BK	W
W	R	P	B	BR	BK	O	Y	G

Pupils may need to be advised that when things go wrong it is usually best to start again from the beginning.

Further Study

					R		W	
BK			R	BR			P	
	P	O					Y	B
G	R				O			
		B						
				W		Y	BR	
W	BK		G					
	Y				B		R	
								O

For enthusiasts, here is another puzzle.

Challenge ρ (rho)
Domino Dilemma

This set of dominoes is not complete!
What is missing?

36

Explanatory Notes: Domino Dilemma

Materials: a set of dominoes with two missing, scissors (optional)
Objectives: to identify the different combinations that make up a set of dominoes

The missing dominoes are 3-4 and double blank

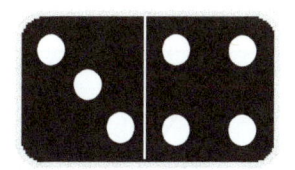

This task is intended to be a practical so that pupils can physically sort the dominoes to identify the missing ones. This can be done by cutting out the dominoes from the task sheet or, better, by using a real set with the two removed. Sets of dominoes are very cheap to buy.

Most pupils will be familiar with sets of dominoes but may not have considered their composition. It will be interesting to observe and share the different sorting strategies that are used. In discussion the mathematical term 'combination' can be introduced.

Further Study

The number of dominoes in a set depends on the numbers used on the dominoes.

This domino is from a set that has the numbers 0-9.

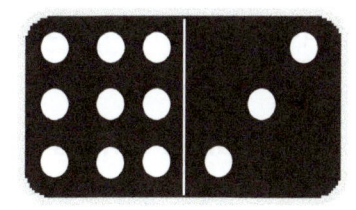

Pupils can investigate the number of dominoes needed for a complete set of 0-9 dominoes and should be able to establish the link with triangular numbers.

Challenge σ (sigma)
Trihexs

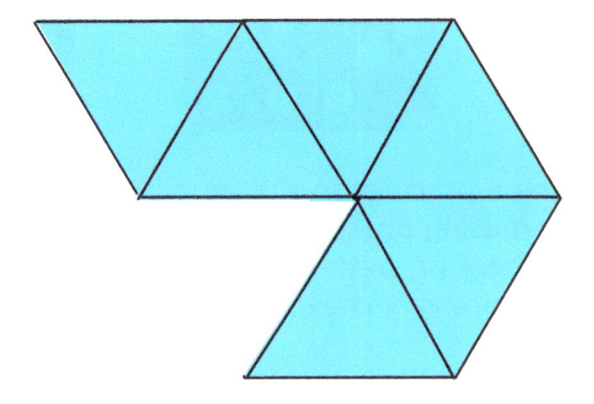

This is a trihex
It is shape made by joining
together (edge to edge)
6 congruent equilateral triangles.

There are 12 different trihexs that can be made by joining 6 congruent equilateral triangles.

Draw all 12 trihexs

Explanatory Notes: Trihexs

Materials: isometric paper (see page 60)
Objectives: to find shapes made from equilateral triangles

Challenge τ (tau)
Sticky Problem

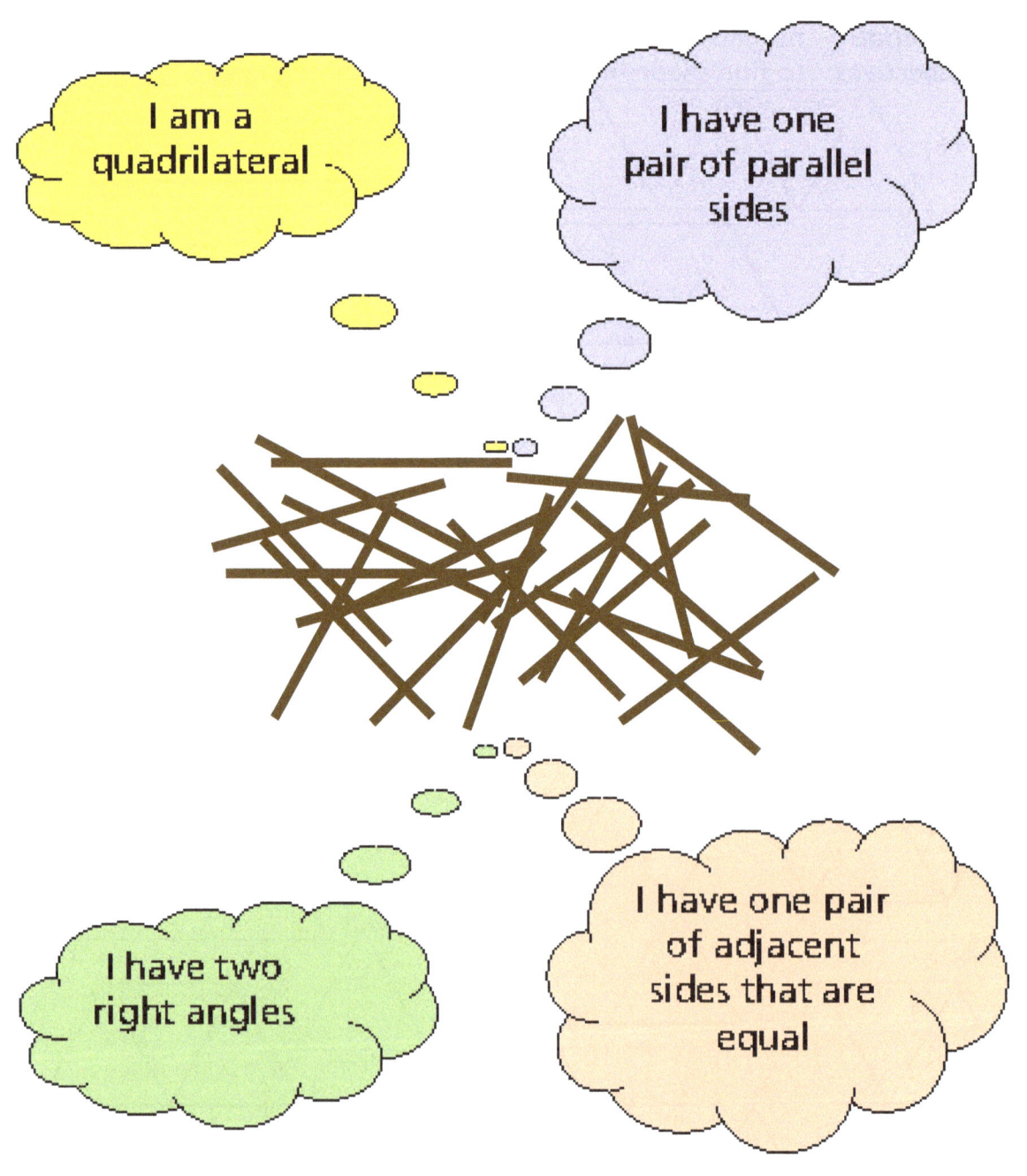

> I am a quadrilateral

> I have one pair of parallel sides

> I have two right angles

> I have one pair of adjacent sides that are equal

Build me using as few sticks as possible

Explanatory Notes: Sticky Problem

Materials: 20 sticks (matchsticks)
Objectives: to accurately construct a quadrilateral given a set of criteria

The clues describe a trapezium similar to those below. Pupils may need to be introduced to the standard symbols for right angles, equal lengths and parallel lines.

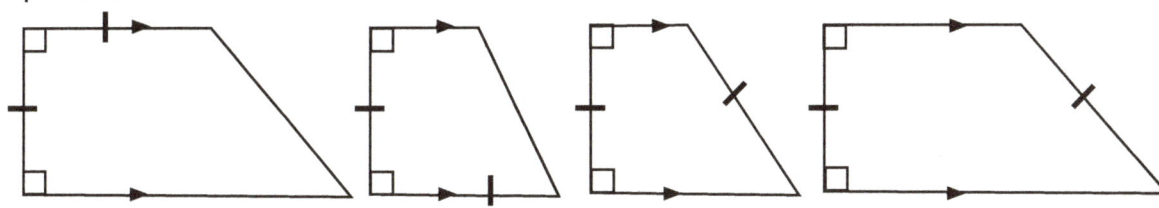

The trapezium can be viewed as a compound shape consisting of a rectangle and a right-angled triangle.

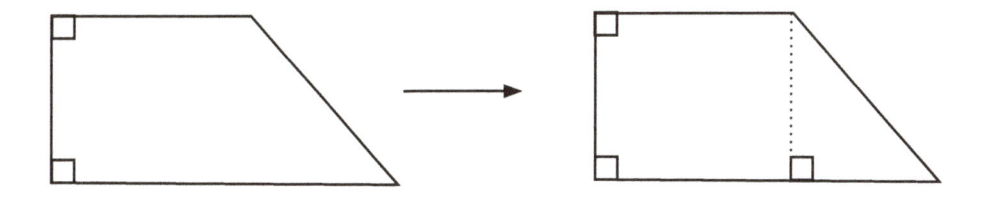

Using sticks, the smallest right-angled triangle that can be constructed is a 3-4-5 triangle. *Some pupils may think that a 2-2-3 will work and will need to be convinced that it won't. They may discover the 3-4-5 property for themselves.*

This leads to the following solutions which B and C use the fewest sticks (14).

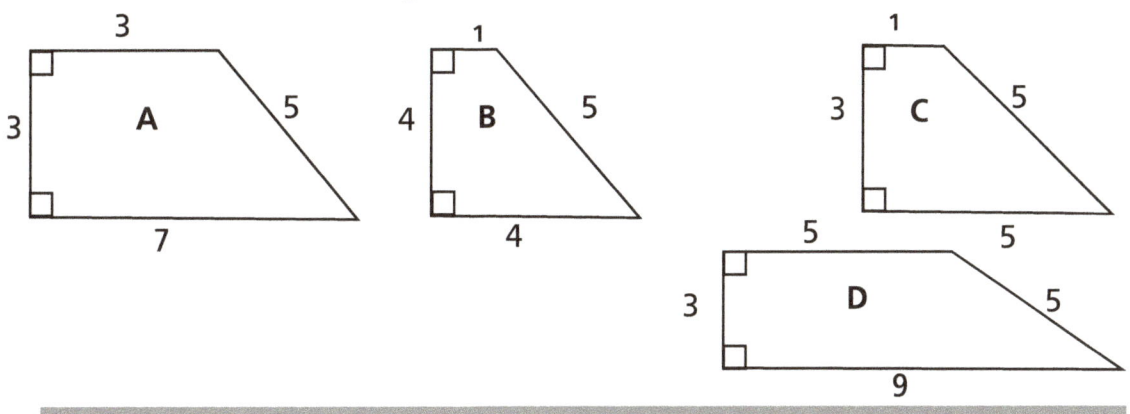

Challenge υ (upsilon)
Star Grid

The **star grid** below is formed by **two** equilateral triangles

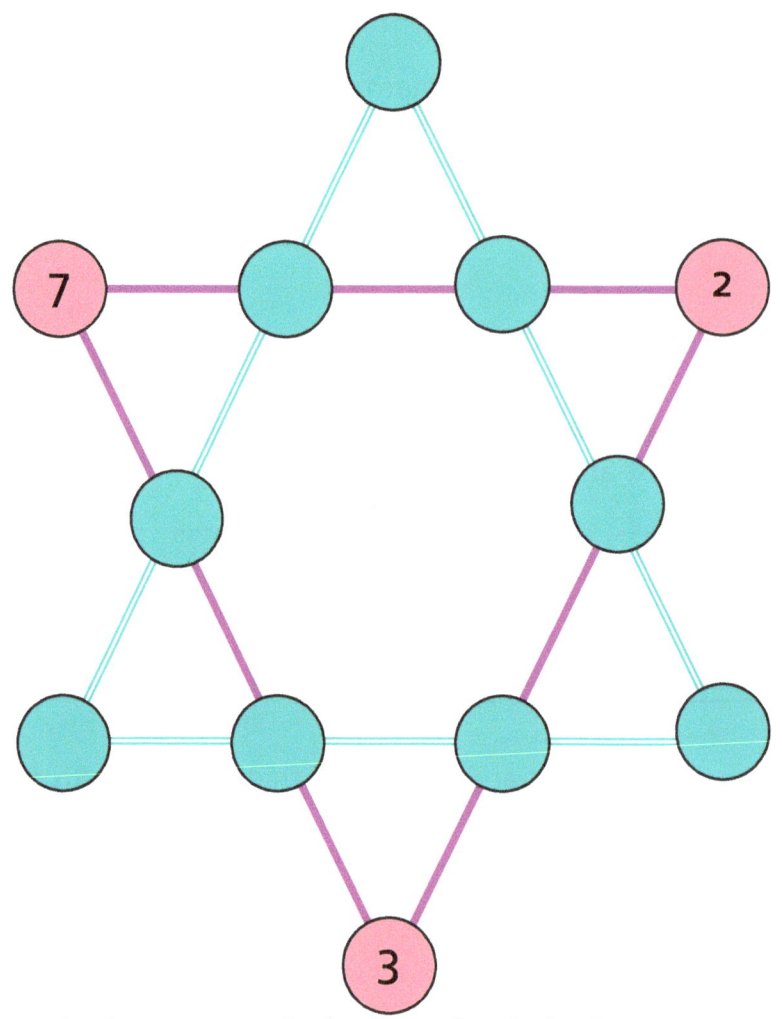

In the pattern, find a line of 4 circles in a row.
Altogether there are six different *lines* of 4 circles
(three in each triangle).

Use a set of counters numbered 1 – 12.

Place the counters 7, 2 and 3 as shown.
Arrange the remaining counters to form the star grid so that
each of the six *lines* has the same sum (total).

Explanatory Notes: Star Grid

Materials: Mastersheet: star grid (see page 57), set of counters 1-12
Objectives: to solve a problem involving the sum of numbers

This problem can be solved using 'pencil & paper' methods. However, for a more practical approach, pupils can use numbered counters on the Star Grid Mastersheet. This approach is easier for 'trial & error'. The solution is:

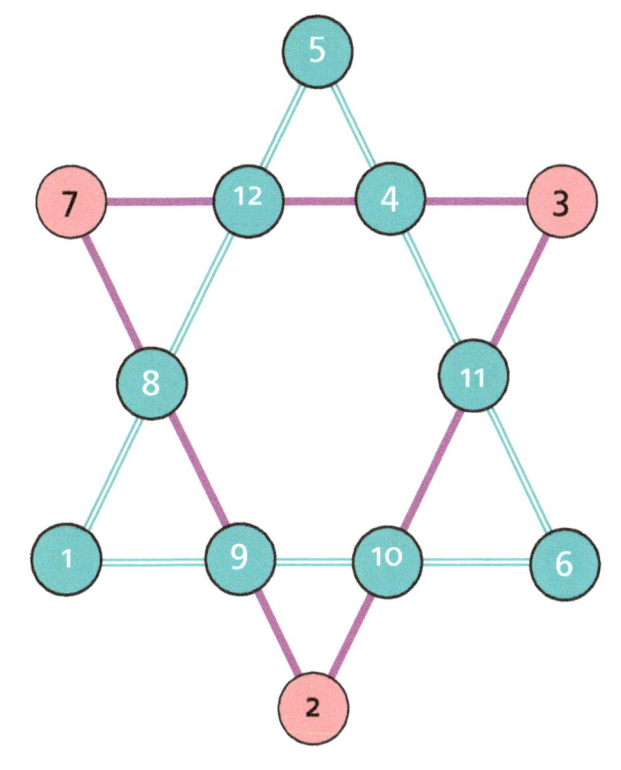

The problem can be made more difficult by *not* giving the position of the 3 numbers (7, 3 & 2) but instead leaving the star grid blank.

Strategy

- The numbers 1-12 add up 78
- Every number appears in two different rows and will count twice.
- The total of all 6 rows is 2 x 78 = 156
- So each row must add up to 156 ÷6 = 26
- Complete the purple triangle first

Challenge φ (phi)
Circle Search

In this grid there are eleven sentences giving you instructions.
Find the sentences, put them in order and follow the instructions.
You will need some plain paper, a sharp pencil, a ruler,
a pair of compasses and a protractor

D	R	A	W	A	C	I	R	C	L	E	O	F	R	A	D	I	U
R	X	B	S	A	S	T	N	I	O	P	N	I	O	J	O	X	S
A	P	R	H	C	A	E	K	R	A	M	Q	R	N	S	T	V	S
W	L	I	G	L	O	M	I	K	Z	U	F	S	C	T	G	S	E
A	A	G	X	N	R	E	R	D	U	K	H	E	J	F	S	M	V
D	B	H	B	M	E	A	S	U	R	E	A	R	C	B	S	O	E
I	E	T	S	C	M	S	O	F		A	E	T	G	L	K	R	N
A	L	A	A	R	I	U	A			W	H	Z	S	I	T	C
M	T	N	E	E	H	R				A	E	E	H	F	E
E	H	G	L	E	L	E					T	T	E	U	Y	N
T	E	L	G	Y	O	C	T			F	J	C	A	O	H	T
E	C	E	N	O	L	H	R	E		G	Q	I	R	R	N	S	I
R	E	F	A	S	K	O	Q	I	W	S	R	H	V	I	S	G	M
A	N	C	D	L	I	R	T	C	C	C	M	D	G	E	C	K	E
B	T	G	N	G	E	D	U	N	U	E	E	V	L	O	A	N	T
C	R	H	I	E	P	B	B	M	P	L	H	I	K	S	T	P	R
O	E	I	F	J	R	S	F	Q	A	C	H	T	H	T	X	R	E
L	O	U	R	G	R	E	E	N	S	E	C	T	O	R	A	O	S

44

Explanatory Notes: Circle Search

Materials: plain paper, sharp pencil, compasses, ruler, protractor
Objectives: to understand and use vocabulary associated with the circle

The task gives an opportunity to explore the definition of the mathematical terms associated with a circle that are found within the search. Discussion might be extended to include other terms such as semicircle, quadrant and segment; and properties such as the right angle in a semicircle and that the tangent is perpendicular to the radius.

The eleven 'hidden' sentences are:

Draw a circle of radius seven centimetres
Mark a point S on the circumference
Join points ASB
Measure chord BS
Draw a tangent to the circle at B
Mark each right angle

Label the centre O
Draw a diameter AB
Find angle ASB
Measure arc BS
Colour green sector AOS

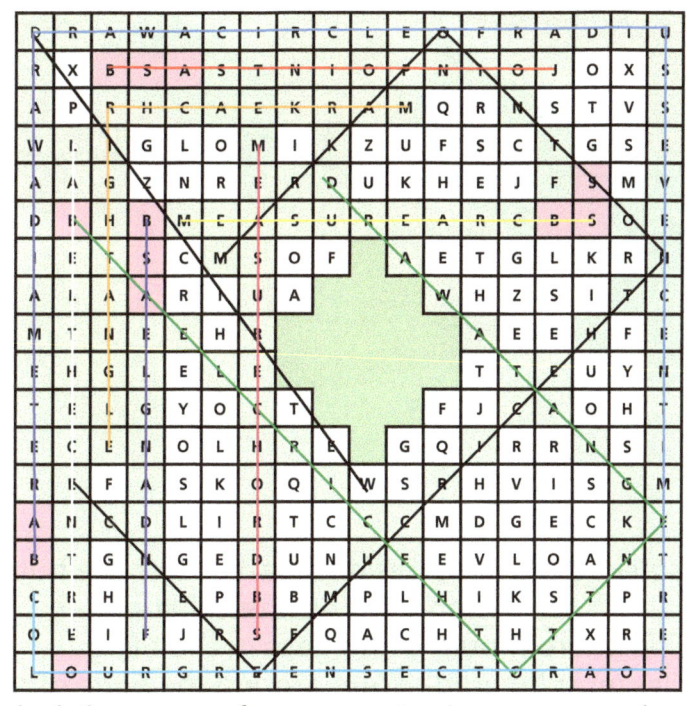

It is important to check the accuracy of measurements using compasses, ruler and protractor and to consider the accuracy of methods for finding the length of an arc (using a piece of string?).

45

Challenge χ (chi)
Tessellating Ts

A new hall is being built at Taddington School.
The hall is to be rectangular and will have floor tiling.
The builder has agreed to use T-shaped tiles for the floor provided the school gives him a tiling pattern to follow.
The pattern will have tiles of three different colours

Use squared paper to design a pattern for the builder.
Your design must be a tessellation.
There should be no gaps in the tiling.
Whole tiles must be used except around the edge of the floor

Explanatory Notes: Tessellating Ts

Materials: squared paper (see page 59), coloured pencils or pens
Objectives: to construct a tessellation

The task offers lots of opportunity for experimentation.
Some more random patterns can work well until a gap is revealed.

Whatever the pattern, it should be clear that it can be extended to fill a large area such as a hall. The pattern below is a simple repeating tessellation which would be fairly easy for the builder to lay. (Note; 3 colours are enough to ensure that no two tiles of the same colour touch)

Challenge ψ (psi)
Cups and Saucers

On the 4x4 grid below are 16 sets of cups (cubes) and saucers (counters). There are 4 matching sets of each of four colours.

Your challenge is to rearrange the sets of cups and saucers so that:
- Every square on the grid has a cup and a saucer
- Every row and every column has one cup of each of the 4 colours
- Every row and every column has one saucer of each colour
- Each of the two diagonals has one saucer and one cup of each colour
- None of the 16 sets are matching
- None of the 16 sets are identical

Explanatory Notes: Cups and Saucers

Materials: a 4x4 grid, 16 cubes (4 of each of four colours) and 16 counters to match.
Objectives: to complete puzzle involving matching pairs

This is a challenging practical puzzle in which 6 success criteria are given. Credit should be given to solutions that match less than 6 of the criteria (for example where one of the diagonals contains more than one of a cup or saucer).

Small cheap plastic cups and saucers in 4 colours are often available from toy shops or online and can add to the practical experience of the task.

The solution below is meets all six criteria.

Possible strategies include arranging the saucers first before adding the cups and ensuring that the diagonals of saucers each contain four different colours before adding the rest of the saucers.

Challenge Ω (omega)
Number Clocks

How to draw the clock pattern for multiples of 6

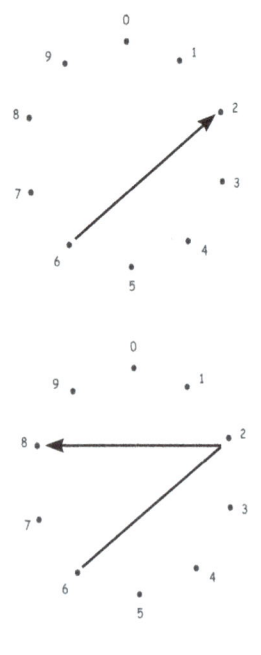

You need a number clock grid, a ruler and a coloured pencil or pen

Think about the 6-times table.
This gives the multiples:
6   12   18   24   30   36   .....

For the clock pattern you only use the last digit of the numbers
<u>6</u>   1<u>2</u>   1<u>8</u>   2<u>4</u>   3<u>0</u>   3<u>6</u>   ....

so you must plot
6 → 2 → 8 → 4 → 0 → 6 → ....

Start at the first number **6**.
Draw a straight line from 6 to 2, then join 2 to 8.

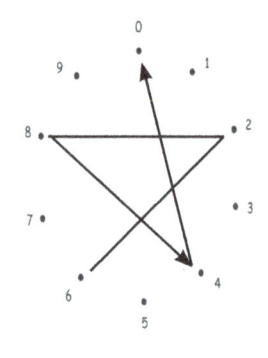

Complete the pattern for the multiples of 6.

Using new circle grids, investigate the clock patterns for the multiples of 2, 3, 4, 5, 7, 8, 9 and 10
(Remember you only use the last digit)

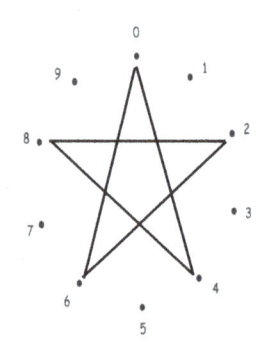

Make the clock patterns for the following sequences:

Square numbers: 1, 4, 9, 16, 25, ...
Cube numbers: 1, 8, 27, 64, ...
Triangular numbers   1, 3, 6, 10, 15, 21, ...
Fibonacci numbers   1, 1, 2, 3, 5, 8, 13, 21, ...

Explanatory Notes: Number Clocks

Materials: Mastersheet: Number Clocks (see page 58), ruler, coloured pencil or pen
Objectives: to investigate circle patterns formed by number sequences.

Here are the patterns for the multiples of:

2 (and its pair 8)
3 (and its pair 7)
4 (and its pair 6)
5

Multiples of 10 stay at zero. Multiples of numbers higher than 10 repeat existing patterns.

More interesting patterns come from:

Square numbers
1, 4, 9, 16, 25, 36 .....

Cube numbers
1, 8, 27, 64, 125, ...

Triangular numbers
1, 3, 6, 10, 15, 21, 28, ...

Fibonacci sequence
1, 1, 2, 3, 5, 8, 13, 21, 34, ...

Remind pupils they only need the last digit in their calculations so the Fibonacci sequence becomes
1, 1, 2, 3, 5, 8, 3, 1, 4, 5, 9, 4, ...

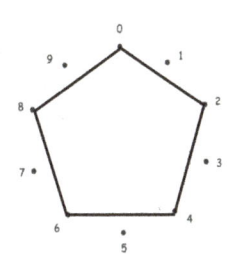

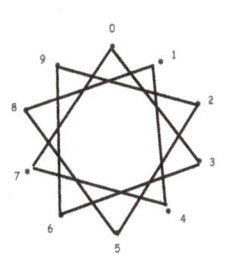

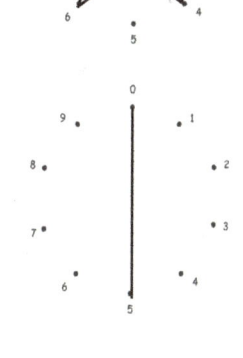

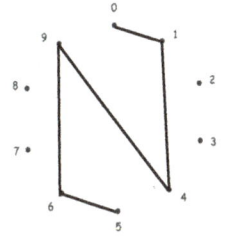

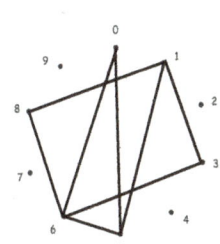

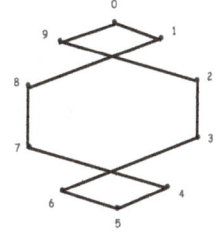

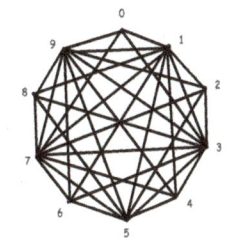

Mastersheet: Detective Work
The Code Dial

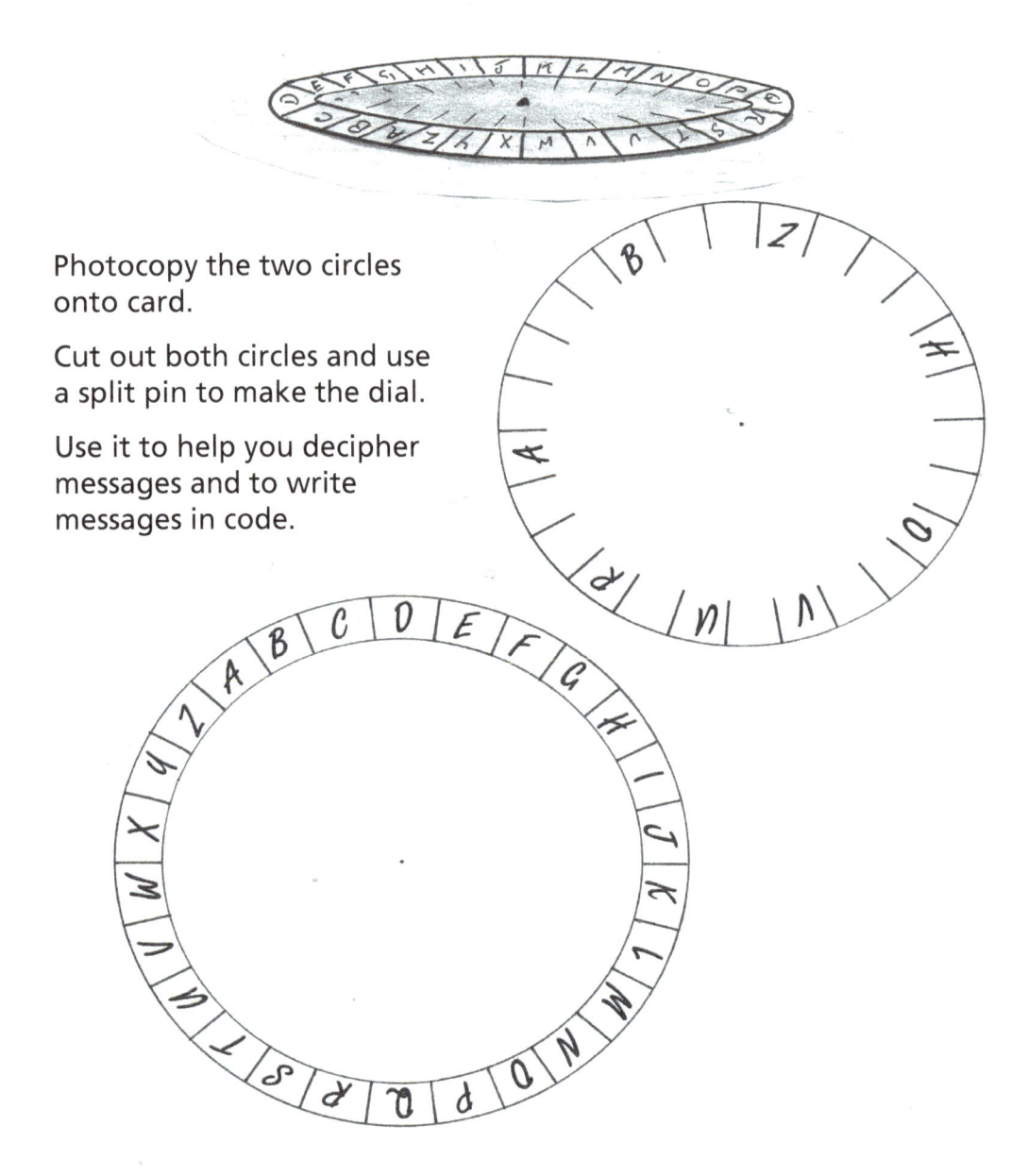

Photocopy the two circles onto card.

Cut out both circles and use a split pin to make the dial.

Use it to help you decipher messages and to write messages in code.

52

Mastersheet: Maze Grids for Maze Corridor

6 x 6 Maze grids

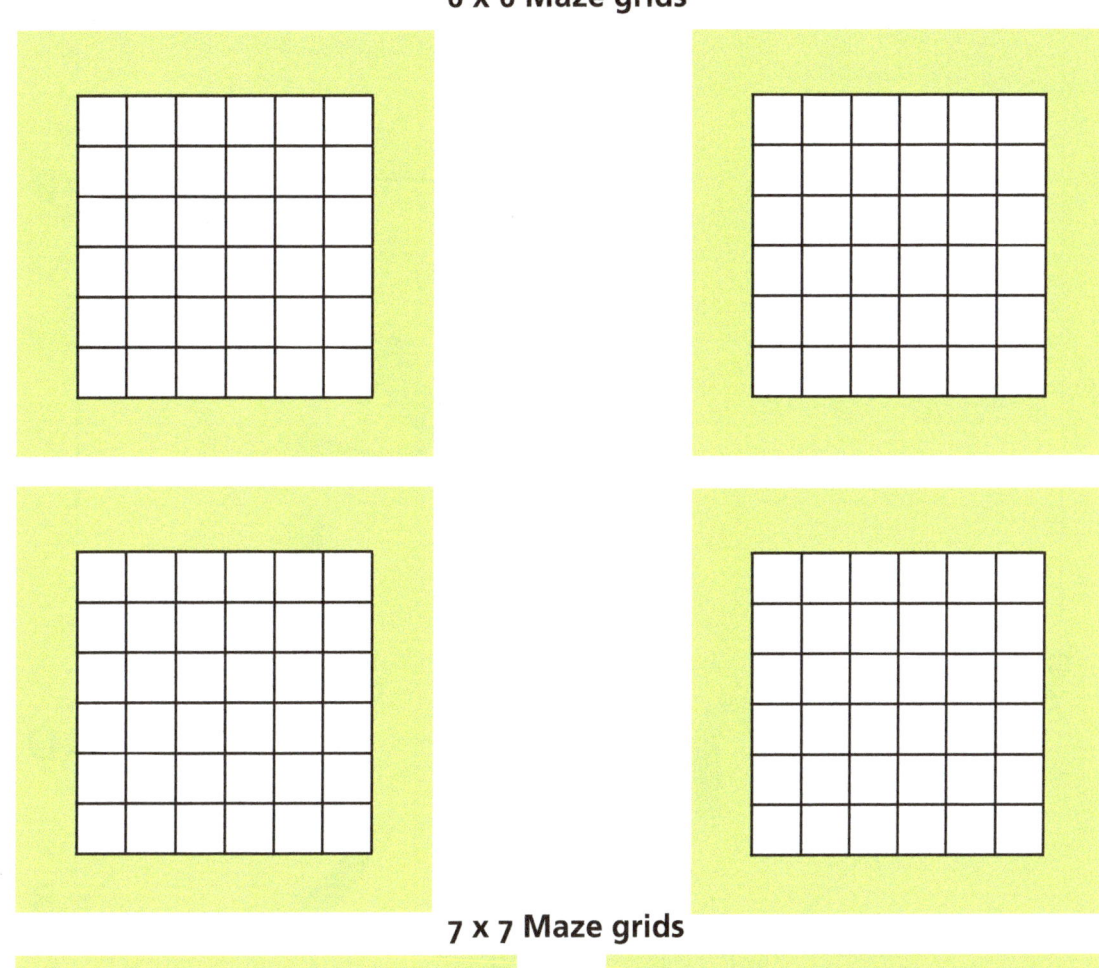

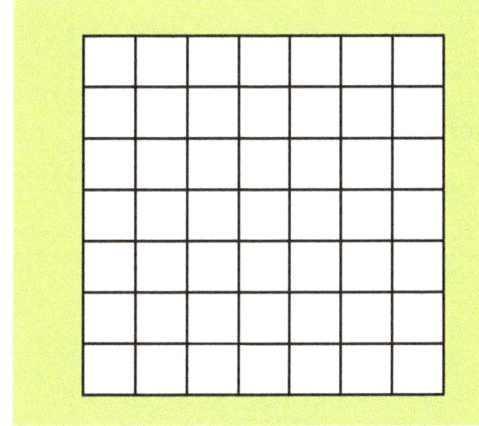

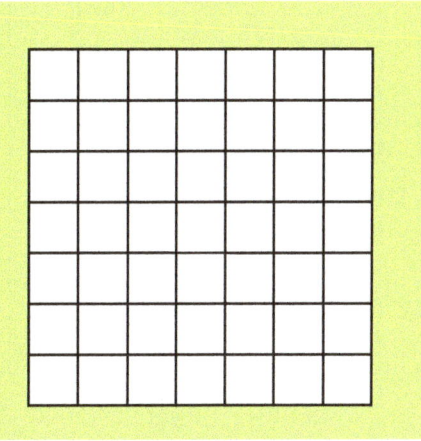

7 x 7 Maze grids

Mastersheet: Nesting
The Kite

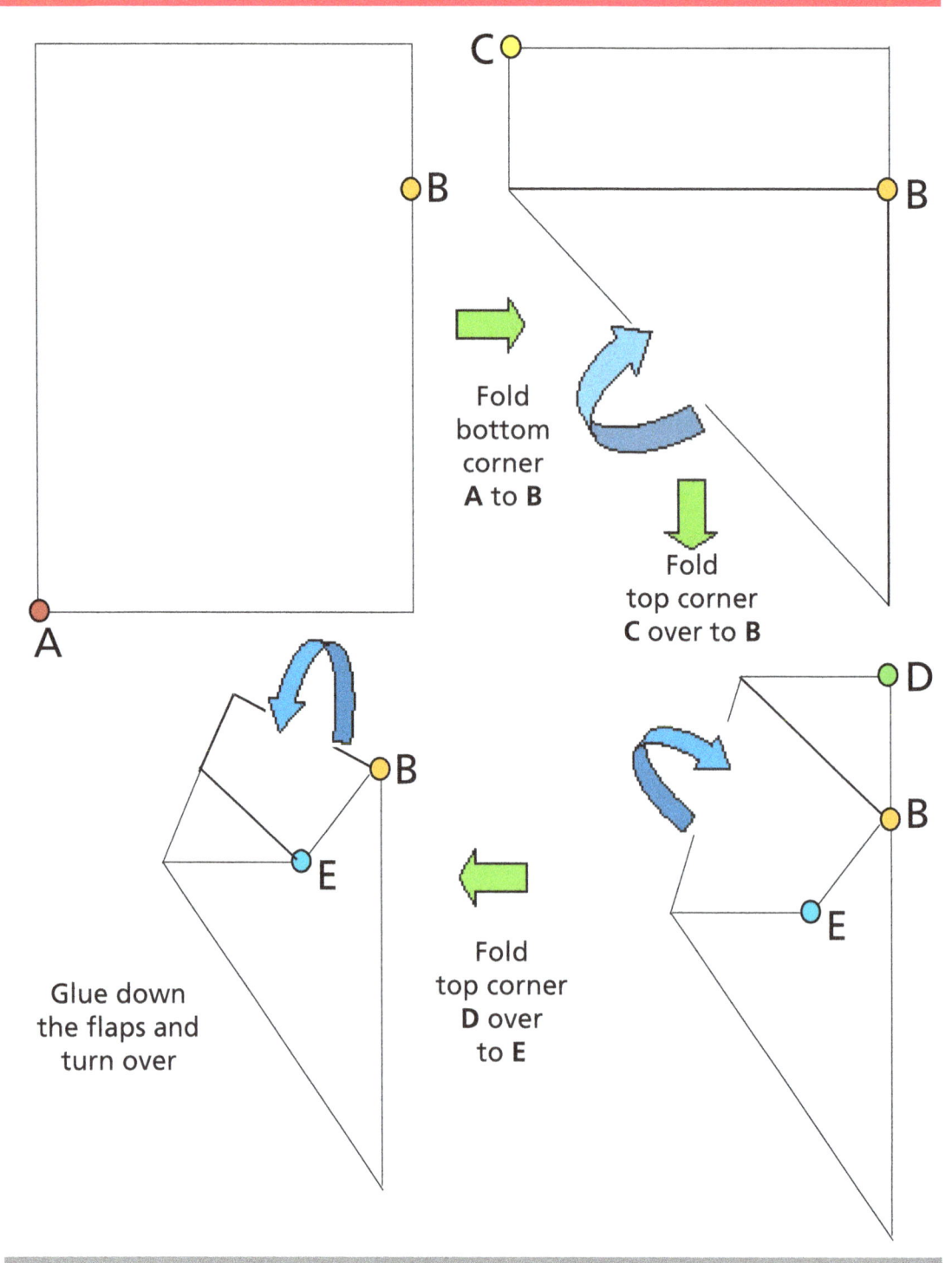

C

B

B

Fold bottom corner **A** to **B**

Fold top corner **C** over to **B**

A

B

E

D

B

E

Glue down the flaps and turn over

Fold top corner **D** over to **E**

54

Mastersheet: Nesting The Equilateral Triangle

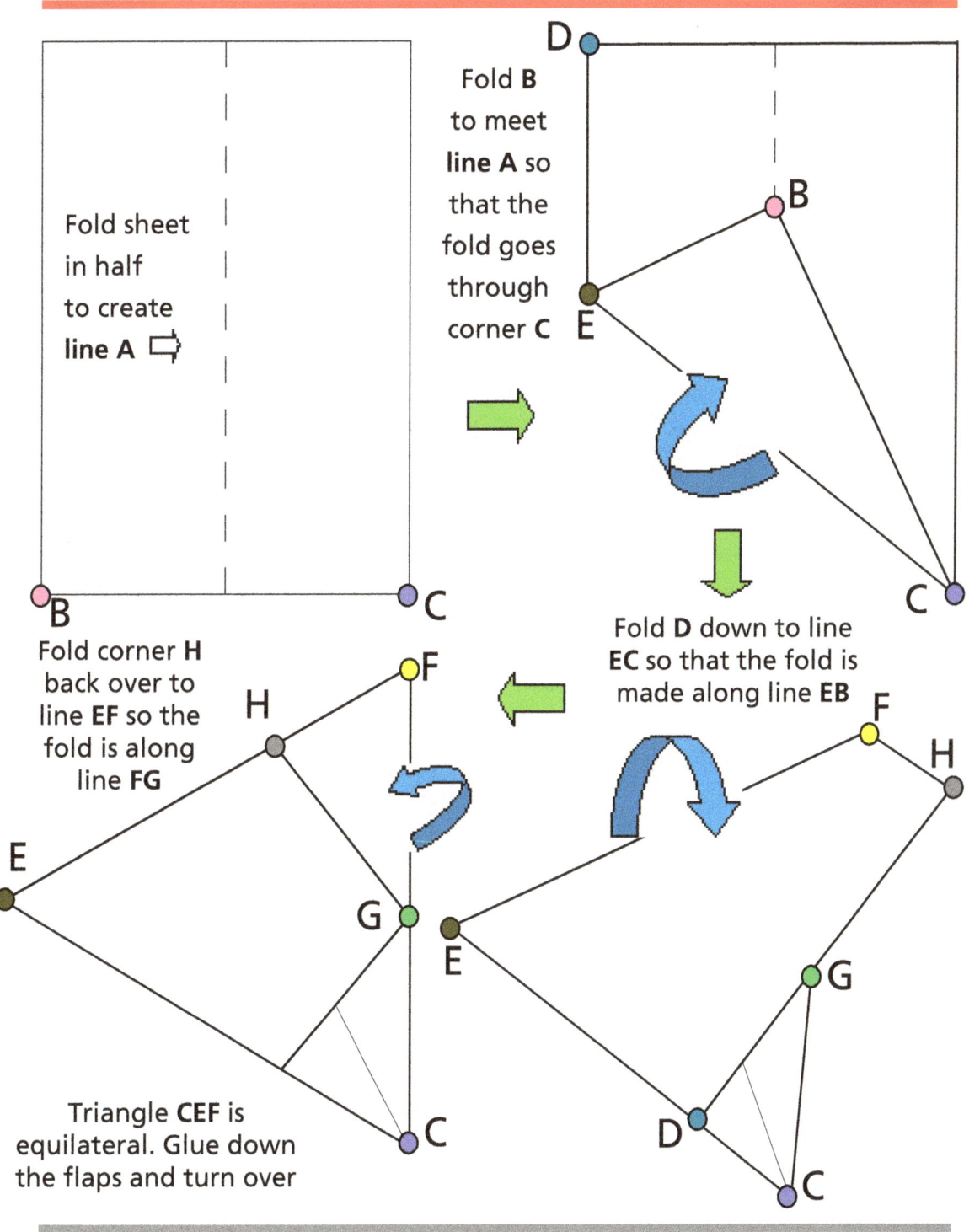

Fold sheet in half to create line A

Fold B to meet line A so that the fold goes through corner C

Fold D down to line EC so that the fold is made along line EB

Fold corner H back over to line EF so the fold is along line FG

Triangle **CEF** is equilateral. Glue down the flaps and turn over

55

Mastersheet: Sudoku Grid for Sudo-Colours

Mastersheet: Star Grid

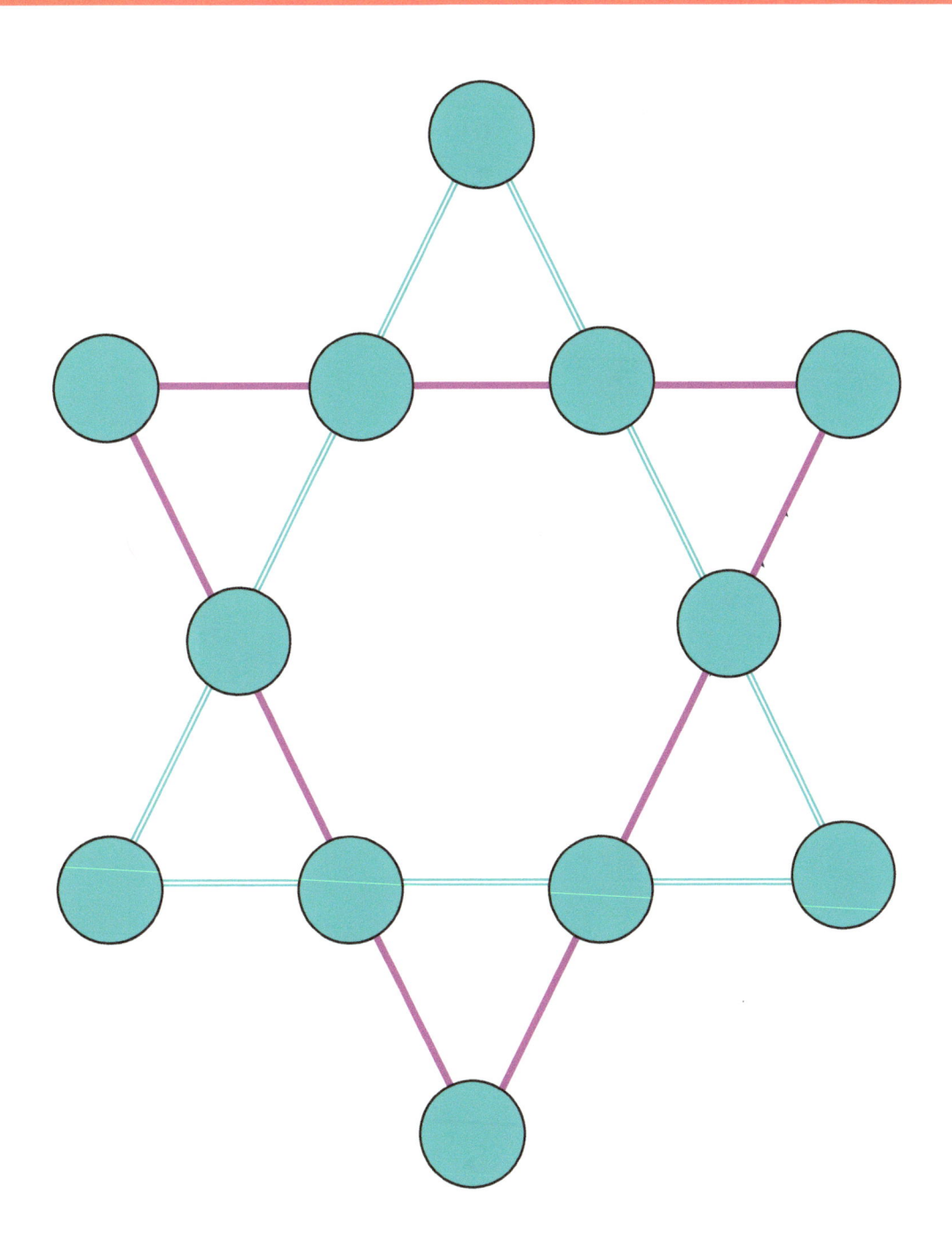

Mastersheet: Number Clocks

```
        0
9           1

8             2


7             3

    6     4
        5


        0
    9       1

8             2


            3

    6     4
        5
```

Squared Paper

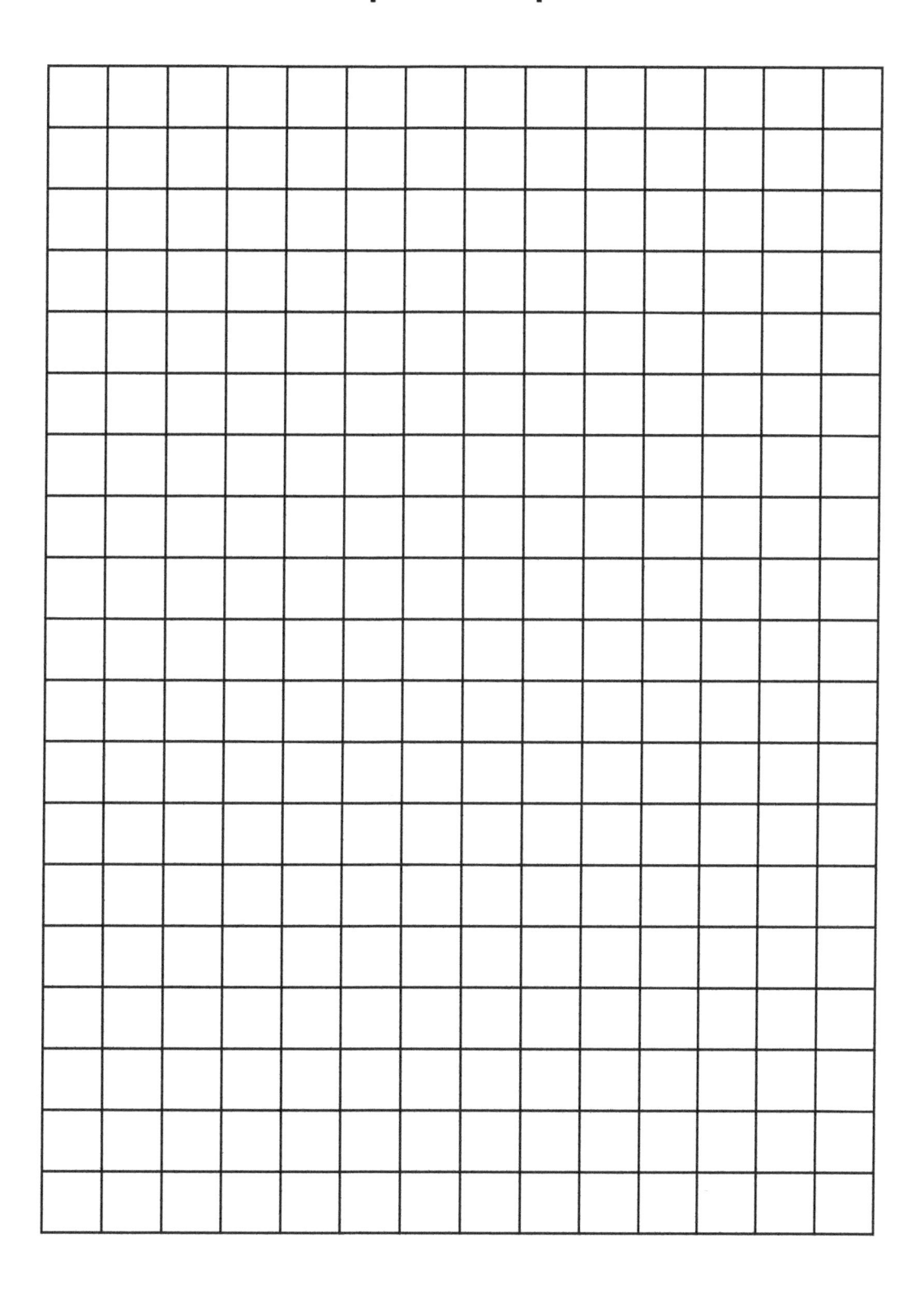

Dotty Isometric Paper

Mathematics Challenge

Certificate of Achievement

Awarded to

....

Signed

....